MW01600278

A Walk of Mercy

The Divine Mercy Stations of the Cross

Written and compiled by

Father Kevin Finnegan

Edited by Sharon Wilson
Photographs by Paul Swenson

Forward by

Bishop Andrew H. Cozzens

†

DEDICATION

To my parents, Patrick and Evelyn, who taught me to say, "I am sorry," and more profoundly, demonstrated how to respond, "I forgive you." In the family with my brother and sister, Kerry and Kathy, I first learned and experienced Divine Mercy.

A Walk of Mercy

CONTENTS

A Walk of Mercy

ACKNOWLEDGMENTS

I extend gratitude to:

Sharon Wilson, without whom this project would not have happened. Her dedicated work, creative vision and persistence worked through obstacles and has made an idea a published reality. Her vision, now come to fruition, will help many others to be inspired towards Divine Mercy.

Paul Swenson, for photographing the Divine Mercy Stations. His photographic technique captures the horrific mystery they point to. Truly his work enhances one's meditation while using this book.

The dedicated staff of Divine Mercy Catholic Church, who kept me focused during my ministry there. In particular, thanks to Mary Beth Purdie, who assisted in the initial drafts of this project.

Divine Mercy of Our Lord Catholic Church in Mesquite, Texas. Their Stations of the Cross derived from the Chaplet of Divine Mercy served to inspire the composition of this book.

Finally, to the artist, who some hundred years ago, painted this Stations of the Cross.

Grateful, simply grateful.

†

The proceeds from the sale of this book will be donated to Divine Mercy
Catholic Church with a portion being set aside for the Garden of Mercy.
The garden is a place of mercy and peace for all who have lost a child.
For more information about the Garden of Mercy see:
www.divinemercy.cc
Divine Mercy Catholic Church
139 Mercy Drive
Faribault, MN 55021

A Walk of Mercy

FORWARD

You are about to embark on a prayerful journey with Jesus which the Church encourages in order to meditate on the passion of Jesus Christ. There are many beautiful meditations on the Stations of the Cross but these stations try to see the passion of Christ as a mystery of mercy. They are being published in the Jubilee Year of Mercy which Pope Francis has declared for the universal Church. You are invited to meditate on Christ's merciful love for you in every station on this journey.

Mercy is the love of God turned towards the sinner. Mercy does not ignore sin, just as Jesus does not ignore sin. Mercy takes sin seriously. Jesus hates sin which is why he enters into the world to conquer it. Jesus loves us so much that he takes upon himself the punishment for our sins. He does this so that we don't have to. The passion is a mystery of mercy because it reveals the depth of Christ's love for us. Christ desires to free us from the punishment of sin which is death. He desires to unite us to himself through pouring out his divine life for us in his passion. Christ loves us as a bridegroom loves his bride; he lays down his life for us. As St. John Chrysostom (†407) said when explaining the depths of Christ sacrificial love for us. He muses to what lengths Christ will go to obtain his bride. Rhetorically, he puts these words in the mouth of Christ: "Even if I have to be covered in spit… even if I have to receive blows, even if I have to go to the cross itself, I will not seek to avoid being crucified in order to obtain my bride."[1] This is mercy. Christ so desires to free us from sin and unite us to himself that he takes on all suffering for us.

Pope Francis points out that the passion is in particular a mystery of mercy. He points out that St. Matthew tells us in his Gospel that before entering into his passion Jesus prayed Psalm 136, the "Great Hallel" psalm which was a part of every Passover celebration. This psalm has the refrain after every line, "For his mercy endures forever." As Pope Francis points out the psalm reveals how "Mercy renders God's history with Israel a history of salvation. To repeat continually "for his mercy endures forever," as the psalm does, seems to break through the dimensions of space and time,

---

[1] Chrysostom, *Third Catechesis* (*Sources Chrétiennes* 366, 214).

inserting everything into the eternal mystery of love. It is as if to say that not only in history, but for all eternity man will always be under the merciful gaze of the Father." He then points out that, "before his Passion, Jesus prayed with this psalm of mercy. Matthew attests to this in his Gospel when he says that, "when they had sung a hymn" (26:30), Jesus and his disciples went out to the Mount of Olives…. Within the very same context of mercy, Jesus entered upon his passion and death, conscious of the great mystery of love that he would consummate on the Cross." (Misercordiae Vultus, 7).

This Walk of Mercy is meant to draw us more deeply into the merciful love of Jesus. It is meant to teach us that our own sufferings and failings are places of mercy not places of condemnation. It is meant to show us that the merciful love of Jesus knows no limits. This is what allows us to surrender our whole lives to him: we know the depth of his mercy for us, so we can pick up our cross and follow him. As you pray these stations and meditate on Jesus mercy poured out for you, I pray you will be able to say in every circumstance what Jesus himself said the night of his passion, "for his mercy endures forever."

Knowing that Jesus himself prayed this psalm makes it even more important for us as Christians, challenging us to take up the refrain in our daily lives by praying these words of praise: "for his mercy endures forever."

†*Most Reverend Andrew H. Cozzens*
January 4, 2016
Auxiliary Bishop of St. Paul and Minneapolis

INTRODUCTION

I have walked the Stations of the Cross, the Via Dolorosa in Jerusalem's Old City on several occasions: early morning before the sun rises and stumbling down the slick gray stone roads; on Friday afternoons as the hot sun beats down with throngs of pilgrims as shop owners and residents go about their routine; and by myself on quiet evenings absorbed with my thoughts, dreams and fears.

Regardless, the Way of the Cross in the Old City always ends at the church of the Holy Sepulcher – and there ultimately pondering not only the crucifixion but the grace of the Resurrection. As you walk these Stations perhaps in your church or the quiet of your room, know that Jesus walks with you – or rather you walk with Him.

This Way of the Cross, these Stations of the Cross, I developed while serving as Pastor of Divine Mercy Catholic Church in Faribault, Minnesota. Privileged to serve these good souls I witnessed their lived faith, often tested but always steadfast and alive. Their faith led the community to forge a new church dedicated to Divine Mercy. This community not only knows Divine Mercy who forgives us our sins. This community expresses Divine Mercy in caring for the needy, poor, imprisoned, immigrant, the youth and the aged. They have a faith always tending toward the hope of our Risen Lord Jesus.

When developing these stations, I came across "Divine Mercy Stations of the Cross" used at Divine Mercy of Our Lord Catholic Church in Mesquite, Texas. Then I incorporated prayers from our tradition. These spiritually rich prayers have helped me and countless people through struggles and fears, have inspired the faithful to love with greater magnanimity, comforted the bereaved and encouraged the sinner. The accompanying pictures were the Stations of the Cross once used at St. Lawrence Catholic Church in Faribault. They now grace the columned walkway around Divine Mercy Catholic Church. Dating from the late 19th century, they were painted in Germany. They are on copper plates which were gold plated, then painted. You can see the glitter of the gold leaf peeking through in some places where the painter didn't fully cover them While not much is known about them, we do know that they beautifully capture the essence of Jesus' Way of the Cross to Calvary.

The Divine Mercy Icon evokes us all to know the tender but robust mercy of God. Jesus has conquered death. He has conquered our sin. He calls us to proclaim his Gospel to all. This Icon expresses the depth of the Divine Mercy Sunday Gospel. As you ponder this Gospel, see the Risen Christ whispering to you and the Church, *peace be with you.*

> On the evening of that first day of the week, when the doors were locked, where the disciples were, for fear of the Jews, Jesus came and stood in their midst and said to them, "Peace be with you." When he had said this, he showed them his hands and his side. The disciples rejoiced when they saw the Lord. Jesus said to them again, "Peace be with you. As the Father has sent me, so I send you." And when he had said this, he breathed on them and said to them, "Receive the holy Spirit. Whose sins you forgive are forgiven them, and whose sins you retain are retained." (John 20:19-23)

The last portion of each station comes from the Stabat Mater. The Stabat Mater is a thirteenth-century Latin hymn which means "the Mother was standing." The hymn consists of twenty couplets which describe the Sorrows of the Blessed Virgin at the Cross.

I pray these words help you to know that Mary, our Mother, walks at our side leading us ever closer to Jesus who is our Mercy.

Father Kevin Finnegan

THE WAY BEGINS

Presider: In the name of the Father, and of the Son and of the Holy Spirit.
All: Amen.

Presider: Lord Jesus, today we lovingly recall your journey to Calvary which fulfilled your promised redemption of our sins.
We remember your willing attitude in carrying your Cross. You endured physical and moral sufferings because of your unconditional love for us. Your sacrificial and merciful love manifests your forgiving heart.
Lord Jesus, as we begin to make the Way of the Cross, we ask you to go before us and lead us to follow your footsteps faithfully. Fill us with sorrow and contrition for our sins. Give us grace to carry our crosses in loving imitation of you.

THE FIRST STATION:
JESUS IS CONDEMNED TO DEATH

Presider: We adore you, O Christ, and we praise you.
(Genuflect)
All: Because by your holy cross you have redeemed the world.

Reader: Pontius Pilate connived with the will of the religious leaders. He sentenced Jesus Christ to death though He was innocent.

Presider: Eternal Father, I offer you the Body and Blood, Soul and Divinity of your dearly beloved Son, our Lord Jesus Christ.
All: In atonement for our sins and those of the whole world.

Presider: We pray together.
(Kneel)
All: In every need let me come to you with humble trust, saying: Jesus, help me!
In all my doubts, perplexities and temptations: Jesus, help me!
In hours of loneliness, weariness and trials: Jesus, help me!
In the failure of my plans and hopes, in disappointments, troubles and sorrows: Jesus, help me!
When others fail me, and your grace alone can assist me: Jesus, help me!
When I throw myself on your tender love as a Father and Savior: Jesus, help me!
When my heart is cast down by failure
at seeing no good come from my efforts: Jesus, help me!
When I feel impatient, and my cross irritates me: Jesus, help me!
When I am ill, and my head and hands cannot work and I am lonely: Jesus, help me!
Always, always, in spite of weakness, falls and shortcomings of every kind: Jesus, help me and never forsake me. Amen.

~Jesus, Help Me Prayer - Anonymous

Presider: For the sake of His being condemned to death.
All: Have mercy on us and on the whole world.

(Stand)
All Sing: At the cross her station keeping,
Mary stood in sorrow weeping,
when her son was crucified.

5

THE SECOND STATION:
JESUS TAKES UP HIS CROSS

Presider: We adore you, O Christ, and we praise you.
(Genuflect)
All: Because by your holy cross you have redeemed the world.

Reader: Jesus accepted His Cross which was too heavy for His frail body.
Christ suffered carrying the heavy Cross to redeem us.

Presider: Eternal Father, I offer You the Body and Blood,
Soul and Divinity of Your dearly beloved Son, our Lord Jesus Christ.
All: In atonement for our sins and those of the whole world.

Presider: We pray together.
(Kneel)
All: Take, O Lord, and receive my entire liberty,
my memory, my understanding and my whole will.
All that I am and all that I possess you have given me:
I surrender it all to you
to be disposed of according to your will.
Give me only your love and your grace;
with these I will be rich enough,
and will desire nothing more.

~St. Ignatius of Loyola, 1491 – 1556

Presider: For the sake of His carrying the cross.
All: Have mercy on us and on the whole world.

(Stand)
All Sing: While she waited in her anguish,
seeing Christ in torment languish,
bitter sorrow pierced her heart.

THE THIRD STATION:
JESUS FALLS THE FIRST TIME

Presider: We adore you, O Christ, and we praise you.
(Genuflect)
All: Because by your holy cross you have redeemed the world.

Reader: Weakened, prodded, cursed, and fallen, His whole Body bruised and swollen, Jesus tripped and lay in pain because of our sins. Dust and blood were seen in His Holy Face when He looked up to heaven asking God the Father to let Him redeem us sinners.

Presider: Eternal Father, I offer you the Body and Blood,
Soul and Divinity of your dearly beloved Son, our Lord Jesus Christ.
All: In atonement for our sins and those of the whole world.

Presider: We pray together.
(Kneel)
All: Behold me, my beloved Jesus,
weighed down under the burden of my trials and sufferings,
I cast myself at your feet, that you may renew my strength and my courage,
while I rest here in your Presence.
Permit me to lay down my cross in your Sacred Heart,
for only your infinite goodness can sustain me;
only your love can help me bear my cross;
only your powerful hand can lighten its weight.
O Divine King, Jesus, whose heart is so compassionate to the afflicted,
I wish to live in you; suffer and die in you.
During my life be to me my model and my support;
at the hour of my death, be my hope and my refuge. Amen.

~Anonymous

Presider: For the sake of His first fall under the weight of the cross.
All: Have mercy on us and on the whole world.

(Stand)
All Sing: With what pain and desolation,
with what noble resignation,
Mary watched her dying Son.

THE FOURTH STATION:
JESUS MEETS HIS SORROWFUL MOTHER

Presider: We adore you, O Christ, and we praise you.
(Genuflect)
All: Because by your holy cross you have redeemed the world.

Reader: There on the road to Calvary, Jesus met His afflicted Mother. They looked at each other's teary eyes. Oh, what sadness our loving Virgin Mother felt in meeting her suffering Son; truly, a sword pierced her heart.

Presider: Eternal Father, I offer you the Body and Blood, Soul and Divinity of your dearly beloved Son, our Lord Jesus Christ.
All: In atonement for our sins and those of the whole world.

Presider: We pray together.
(Kneel)
All: Holy Mary, Mother of God, preserve in me the heart of a child, pure and transparent as a spring.
Obtain for me a simple heart that does not brood over sorrows;
A heart generous in giving itself,
Quick to feel compassion;
A faithful, generous heart that forgets no favor and holds no grudge.
Give me a humble, gentle heart.
Loving without asking any return;
A great indomitable heart, that no ingratitude can close,
No indifference can weary;
A heart tortured by its desire for the glory of Jesus Christ.
Pierced by His love –
With a wound that will heal only in heaven. Amen.
~*Prayer for the Heart of a Child, Léonce de Grandmaison, 1868-1927*

Presider: For the sake of His meeting His sorrowful mother.
All: Have mercy on us and on the whole world.

(Stand)
All Sing: Ever patient in her yearning,
though her tear-filled eyes were burning,
Mary gazed upon her Son.

11

THE FIFTH STATION:
SIMON OF CYRENE CARRIES THE CROSS

Presider: We adore you, O Christ, and we praise you.
(Genuflect)
All: Because by your holy cross you have redeemed the world.

Reader: On their way out they met a Cyrenian named Simon; this man they pressed into service to carry the cross.

~Matthew 27:32

Presider: Eternal Father, I offer you the Body and Blood, Soul and Divinity of your dearly beloved Son, our Lord Jesus Christ
All: In atonement for our sins and those of the whole world.

Presider: We pray together.
(Kneel)
All: God has created me to do him some definite service;
He has committed some work to me,
which he has not committed to another.
I have my mission;
I may never know it in this life, but I shall be told it in the next.
I have a part in a great work;
I am a link in a chain, a bond of connection between persons.
He has not created me for naught.
I shall do good, I shall do His work;
I shall be an angel of peace,
a preacher of truth in my own place,
while not intending it,
if I do but keep His commandments
and serve Him in my calling.

~I Have a Mission, Blessed John Henry Newman, 1801 – 1890

Presider: For the sake of His accepting help in carrying the cross.
All: Have mercy on us and on the whole world.

(Stand)
All Sing: Who, that sorrow contemplating,
on that passion meditating,
would not share the Virgin's grief.

THE SIXTH STATION:
VERONICA WIPES THE FACE OF JESUS

Presider: We adore you, O Christ, and we praise you.
(Genuflect)
All: Because by your holy cross you have redeemed the world.

Reader: Veronica hastily went near Jesus and wiped His face with a piece of cloth. The face of Jesus was imprinted in the cloth.

Presider: Eternal Father, I offer you the Body and Blood, Soul and Divinity of your dearly beloved Son, our Lord Jesus Christ.
All: In atonement for our sins and those of the whole world.

Presider: We pray together.
(Kneel)
All: Lord, make me an instrument of Your peace.
Where there is hatred, let me sow love;
where there is injury, pardon;
where there is doubt, faith;
where there is despair, hope;
where there is darkness, light;
where there is sadness, joy.
O, Divine Master,
grant that I may not so much seek to be consoled as to console;
to be understood as to understand;
to be loved as to love.
For it is in giving that we receive;
it is in pardoning that we are pardoned;
it is in dying that we are born again to eternal life.
~Attributed to Saint Francis of Assisi, 1181 – 1226

Presider: For the sake of His receiving mercy from Veronica.
All: Have mercy on us and on the whole world.

(Stand)
All Sing: Christ she saw, for our salvation,
scourged with cruel acclamation,
bruised and beaten by the rod.

THE SEVENTH STATION:
JESUS FALLS THE SECOND TIME

Presider: We adore you, O Christ, and we praise you.
(Genuflect)
All: Because by your holy cross you have redeemed the world.

Reader: Again, under the weight of the cross Jesus falls to the pavement. His pain and suffering we cannot fathom.

Presider: Eternal Father, I offer you the Body and Blood, Soul and Divinity of your dearly beloved Son, our Lord Jesus Christ.
All: In atonement for our sins and those of the whole world.

Presider: We pray together.
(Kneel)
All: My Lord God, I have no idea where I am going.
I do not see the road ahead of me.
I cannot know for certain where it will end.
Nor do I really know myself, and the fact that
I think I am following your will does not mean that I am actually doing so.
But I believe that the desire to please you does in fact please you.
And I hope I have that desire in all that I am doing.
I hope that I will never do anything apart from that desire.
And I know that if I do this you will lead me by the right road
though I may know nothing about it.
Therefore, will I trust you always
though I may seem to be lost and in the shadow of death.
I will not fear, for you are ever with me,
and you will never leave me to face my perils alone.
~ Thomas Merton, 1915 – 1968, Thoughts in Solitude

Presider: For the sake of His second fall under the weight of the cross.
All: Have mercy on us and on the whole world.

(Stand)
All Sing: Christ she saw with life-blood failing,
all her anguish unavailing,
saw him breathe his very last.

THE EIGHTH STATION:
JESUS MEETS THE WOMEN OF JERUSALEM

Presider: We adore you, O Christ, and we praise you.
(Genuflect)
All: Because by your holy cross you have redeemed the world.

Reader: A great crowd of people followed Him, including women who beat their breasts and lamented over Him. Jesus turned to them and said, "Daughters of Jerusalem, do not weep for me. Weep for yourselves and for your children." *~Luke 23:27-28*

Presider: Eternal Father, I offer you the Body and Blood, Soul and Divinity of your dearly beloved Son, our Lord Jesus Christ.
All: In atonement for our sins and those of the whole world.

Presider: We pray together.
(Kneel)
All: Lord, human love helps me to understand divine love.
Human love at its best, unselfish, glowing, illuminating our days,
gives us a glimpse of the love of God for man.
Love is the best thing we can know in this life,
but it must be sustained by an effort of the will.
It must lie still and quiet, dull and smoldering, for periods.
It grows through suffering and patience and compassion.
We must suffer for those we love,
we must endure their traits and their suffering,
we must even take upon ourselves the penalties due their sins.
Thus we learn to understand the love of God for His creatures.
Thus we understand the crucifixion.
~Dorothy Day, 1897 – 1980, From Union Square to Rome, Published by the Preservation of the Faith Press, 1938

Presider: For the sake of His consoling the women.
All: Have mercy on us and on the whole world.

(Stand)
All Sing: Mary, fount of love's devotion,
let me share with true emotion
all the sorrow you endured.

THE NINTH STATION:
JESUS FALLS THE THIRD TIME

Presider: We adore you, O Christ, and we praise you.
(Genuflect)
All: Because by your holy cross you have redeemed the world.

Reader: Jesus falls the third time. Exhausted by carrying his cross - carrying our sins and failures - Jesus experiences the burden of the heavy cross.

Presider: Eternal Father, I offer you the Body and Blood, Soul and Divinity of your dearly beloved Son, our Lord Jesus Christ.
All: In atonement for our sins and those of the whole world.

Presider: We pray together.
(Kneel)
All: Lord, teach me to be generous,
teach me to serve you as I should,
to give and not to count the cost,
to fight and not to heed the wounds,
to toil and not to seek for rest,
to labor and ask not for reward,
save that of knowing that I do your most holy will.
                                    ~St. Ignatius of Loyola, 1491 – 1556

Presider: For the sake of His third fall under the weight of the cross yet persevering to Calvary.
All: Have mercy on us and on the whole world.

(Stand)
All Sing: Virgin, ever interceding,
hear me in my fervent pleading:
Fire me with your love of Christ.

THE TENTH STATION:
JESUS IS STRIPPED OF HIS GARMENTS

Presider: We adore you, O Christ, and we praise you.
(Genuflect)
All: Because by your holy cross you have redeemed the world.

Reader: When they reached the place called Golgotha which means skull, they offered Him wine mixed with gall. Jesus tasted it but would not take it. His blood dripped as His sticking wounds opened when they tore off His clothes.

Presider: Eternal Father, I offer you the Body and Blood, Soul and Divinity of your dearly beloved Son, our Lord Jesus Christ.
All: In atonement for our sins and those of the whole world.

Presider: We pray together.
(Kneel)
All: In the terrible desert of life,
O my sweetest Jesus,
Protect souls from disaster,
For You are the Fountain of Mercy.
Let the resplendence of your rays,
O sweet Commander of our souls,
Let mercy change the world.
And you who have received this grace, serve Jesus.
Steep is the great highway I must travel,
But I fear nothing,
For the pure fount of mercy is flowing for my sake,
And, with it, strength for the humble soul.
I am exhausted and worn out,
But my conscience bears me witness
That I do all for the greater glory of the Lord,
The Lord who is my repose and my heritage.
                    ~Diary of Saint Faustina; 1000, St. Faustina Kowalska, 1905-1938

Presider: For the sake of His being stripped.
All: Have mercy on us and on the whole world.
(Stand)

All Sing: Mother, may this prayer be granted:
That Christ's love may be implanted
in the depths of my poor soul.

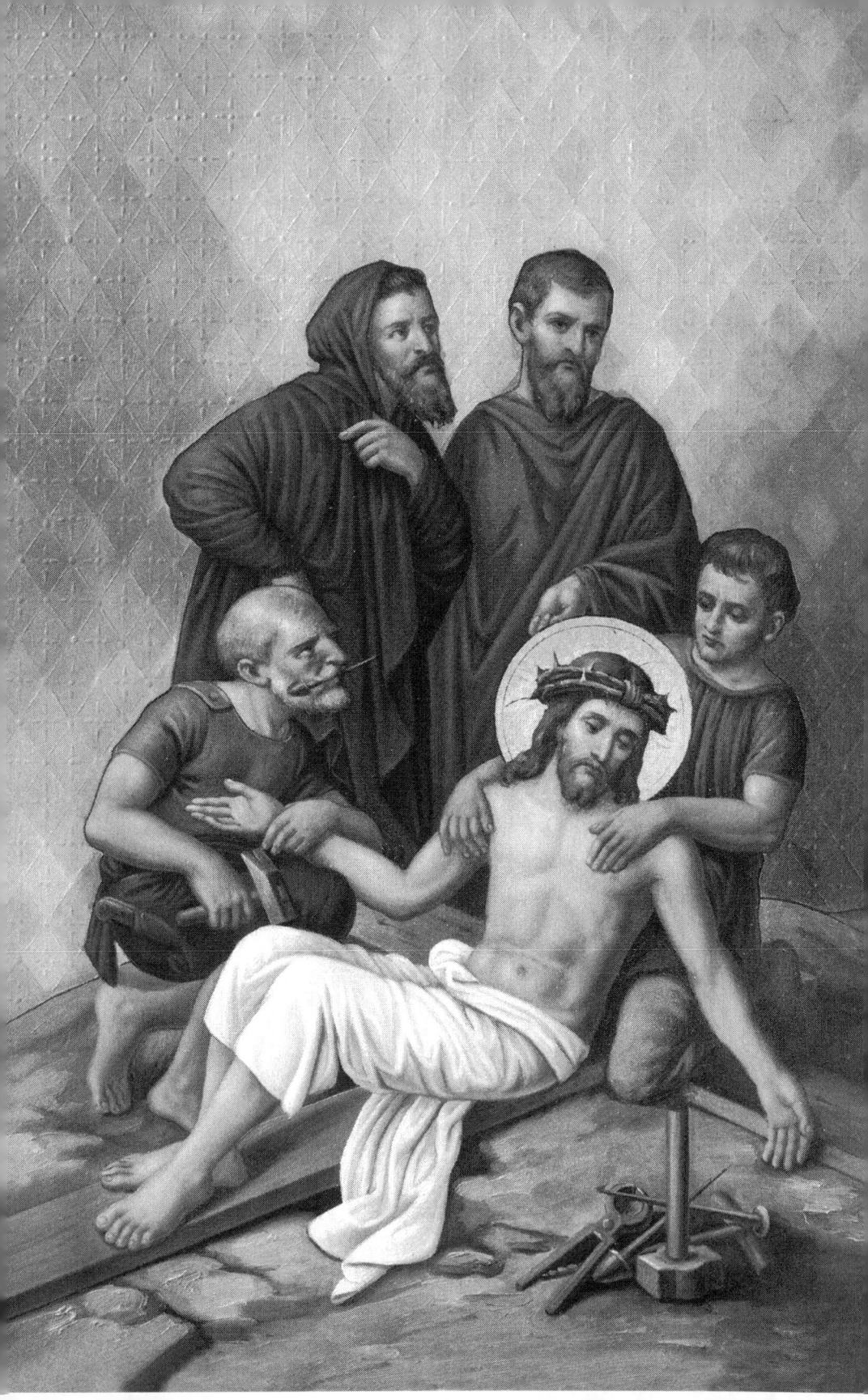

THE ELEVENTH STATION:
JESUS IS NAILED TO THE CROSS

Presider: We adore you, O Christ, and we praise you.
(Genuflect)
All: Because by your holy cross you have redeemed the world.

Reader: When they came to Golgotha, they crucified Jesus and the two criminals, one on His right and the other on His left. And Jesus said, "Father, forgive them, for they know not what they do."

~*Luke 23:33-34; Jn19:18*

Presider: Eternal Father, I offer you the Body and Blood, Soul and Divinity of your dearly beloved Son, our Lord Jesus Christ.
All: In atonement for our sins and those of the whole world.

Presider: We pray together.
(Kneel)
All: Soul of Christ, make me holy.
Body of Christ, save me.
Blood of Christ, fill me with love.
Water from Christ's side, wash me.
Passion of Christ, strengthen me.
Good Jesus, hear me.
Within your wounds, hide me.
Never let me be parted from you.
From the evil enemy, protect me.
At the hour of my death, call me,
and tell me to come to you that with your saints
I may praise you through all eternity. Amen.

~*Anima Christi, Blessed Bernardino of Feltre, 1439-1494*

Presider: For the sake of His being crucified.
All: Have mercy on us and on the whole world.

All Sing: At the cross, your sorrow sharing,
all your grief and torment bearing,
let me stand and mourn with you.

25

THE TWELFTH STATION:
JESUS DIES UPON THE CROSS

Presider: We adore you, O Christ, and we praise you.
(Genuflect)

All: Because by your holy cross you have redeemed the world.
Presider: Please kneel.

Reader: It was now about twelve o'clock noon, and there was darkness over the whole land until three o'clock in the afternoon. And Jesus cried out in a loud voice, *"Eli, Eli, lema sabachthani?"*, that is, *"My God, my God, why have You forsaken me?"* ... Jesus, again crying out in a loud voice, *"Father, into Thy hands I commend my Spirit!"* and He yielded up His spirit.

~Matthew 27: 45-50

Presider: Eternal Father, I offer you the Body and Blood, Soul and Divinity of your dearly beloved Son, our Lord Jesus Christ.
All: In atonement for our sins and those of the whole world.

Presider: We pray together.
(Remain Kneeling)

All: Father, I abandon myself into your hands; do with me what you will.
Whatever you may do, I thank you: I am ready for all, I accept all.
Let only your will be done in me, and in all your creatures.
I wish no more than this, O Lord.
Into your hands I commend my soul;
I offer it to you with all the love of my heart, for I love you, Lord,
and so need to give myself, to surrender myself into your hands,
without reserve, and with boundless confidence, for you are my Father.

~Blessed Charles de Foucauld, 1858-1916

Presider: For the sake of His death on the cross.
All: Have mercy on us and on the whole world.

(Stand)
All Sing: Fairest maid of all creation,
queen of hope and consolation,
let me feel your grief sublime.

THE THIRTEENTH STATION:
JESUS IS TAKEN DOWN FROM THE CROSS

Presider: We adore you, O Christ, and we praise you.
(Genuflect)
All: Because by your holy cross you have redeemed the world.

Reader: When the soldiers came to Jesus, they saw that He was already dead so that they did not break His legs, but one of them opened His side with a lance, and immediately there came out Blood and Water. The body of Jesus was then taken down from the Cross and laid in the arms of His sorrowful mother.

~John 19:34, 38

Presider: Eternal Father, I offer you the Body and Blood, Soul and Divinity of your dearly beloved Son, our Lord Jesus Christ.
All: In atonement for our sins and those of the whole world.

Presider: We pray together.
(Kneel)
All: You expired, Jesus, but the source of life gushed forth for souls, and the ocean of mercy opened up for the whole world.
O Fount of Life, unfathomable Divine Mercy,
envelop the whole world and empty yourself out upon us.
O Blood and Water, which gushed forth from the Hearth of Jesus
as a fount of mercy for us,
I trust in you.

~Three O'Clock Prayer of Divine Mercy, Diary of St. Faustina; 1319,
St. Faustina Kowalska, 1905-1938

Presider: For the sake of His sorrowful Passion.
All: Have mercy on us and on the whole world.

(Stand)
All Sing: Virgin, in your love befriend me,
at the Judgment Day defend me.
Help me by your constant prayer.

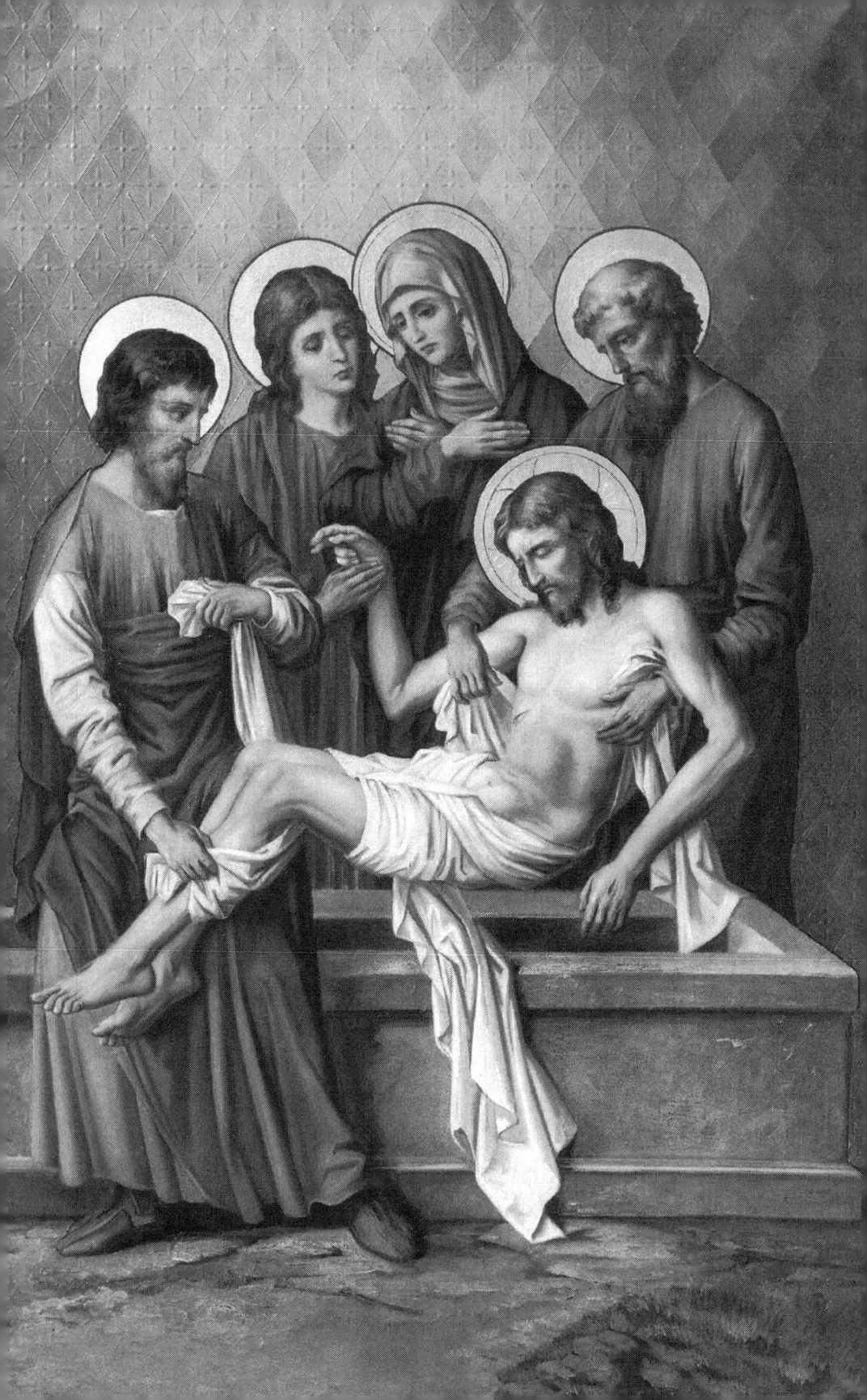

THE FOURTEENTH STATION:
JESUS IS BURIED IN THE TOMB

Presider: We adore you, O Christ, and we praise you.
(Genuflect)
All: Because by your holy cross you have redeemed the world.

Reader: Taking the body of Jesus, Joseph wrapped it in fresh linen and laid it in his own new tomb that had been hewn from a formation of rock. Then he rolled a huge stone across the entrance of the tomb and went away.
~*Matthew 27:59-60*

Presider: Eternal Father, I offer you the Body and Blood, Soul and Divinity of your dearly beloved Son, our Lord Jesus Christ.
All: In atonement for our sins and those of the whole world.

Presider: We pray together.
(Kneel)
All: Although it is not easy to live in constant agony,
to be nailed to the cross of various pains,
still, I am inflamed with love by loving,
And like a Seraph I love God, though I am but weakness.
Oh, great is the soul that, midst suffering,
stands faithfully by God and does His will
and remains uncomforted midst great rainbows and storms,
For God's pure love sweetens her fate.
It is no great thing to love God in prosperity
and thank Him when all goes well,
but rather to adore Him midst great adversities
And love Him for His own sake and place one's hope in Him.
When the soul is in the shadows of Gethsemane,
All alone in the bitterness of pain,
It ascends toward the heights of Jesus,
and though ever drinking bitterness – it is not sad.
~*Diary of St. Faustina: 995, St. Faustina Kowalska, 1905-1938*

Presider: For the sake of His being laid in the tomb.
All: Have mercy on us and on the whole world.

(Stand)
All Sing: Savior, when my life shall leave me,
through your mother's prayers receive me
with the fruits of victory.

31

THE FIFTEENTH STATION:
THE RESURRECTION

Presider: We adore you, O Christ, and we praise you.
(Genuflect)
All: Because by your holy cross you have redeemed the world.

Reader: But at daybreak on the first day of the week they took the spices they had prepared and went to the tomb. They found the stone rolled away from the tomb; but when they entered, they did not find the body of the Lord Jesus. While they were puzzling over this, behold, two men in dazzling garments appeared to them. They were terrified and bowed their faces to the ground. They said to them, "Why do you seek the living one among the dead? He is not here, but he has been raised."

~Luke 24:1-6

Presider: Eternal Father, I offer You the Body and Blood, Soul and Divinity of Your dearly beloved Son, our Lord Jesus Christ.
All: In atonement for our sins and those of the whole world.

Presider: We pray together.
(Kneel)
All: On the evening of that first day of the week, when the doors were locked, where the disciples were, for fear of the Jews, Jesus came and stood in their midst and said to them, "Peace be with you." When he had said this, he showed them his hands and his side. The disciples rejoiced when they saw the Lord. Jesus said to them again, "Peace be with you. As the Father has sent me, so I send you." And when he had said this, he breathed on them and said to them, "Receive the holy Spirit. Whose sins you forgive are forgiven them, and whose sins you retain are retained."

~John 20:19-23

Presider: For the sake of His being raised from the dead.
All: Have mercy on us and on the whole world.

(Stand)
All Sing: Let me to your love be taken,
let my soul in death awaken
to the joys of Paradise.

CLOSING

Presider: Holy God, Holy Mighty One, Holy Immortal One,
All: Have mercy on us and on the whole world.

Presider: Holy God, Holy Mighty One, Holy Immortal One,
All: Have mercy on us and on the whole world.

Presider: Holy God, Holy Mighty One, Holy Immortal One,
All: Have mercy on us and on the whole world.

    Jesus, I trust in you.
    Jesus, I trust in you.
    Jesus, I trust in you.

Presider: In the name of the Father, and of the Son and of the Holy Spirit.
All: Amen.

Postscript
The Divine Mercy Icon
by Sharon Wilson

Sacred Art and Icons

In the rich Roman Catholic tradition, we are accustomed to seeing sacred art in our parishes. Stained glass windows, statues, and paintings depicting the life of Jesus, the apostles, the Holy Family, and saints adorn our churches, chapels and homes. The rich beauty of these items offer us an opportunity for a deepening of prayer through the stories they tell.

Icons are different, not only in technique and style, but in substance. Traditionally a form taken up in the Eastern Catholic Church, icons come with a unique tradition of their own. Using a strict code or method for creating icons, iconographers are said to "write" icons, not paint them. Using traditional materials such as egg tempera paint and gold leaf, they are required to pray and fast while creating an icon. The image itself is not a "realistic" image in the way a great painting might be viewed, but they offer us a way to the "real" Christ and a portal to prayer.

Because they are "written" we are invited to "read" them. Reading an icon is much like reading sacred scripture. We all know that reading spiritual books is good for the soul and our spiritual life, but we also know that reading scripture is different - it is a gateway to God. Words have a special meaning in our faith.

Reflect on John Chapter 1:1
   In the beginning was the Word, and the Word was with God, and the Word was God.

Reflect on what it means to say, "the Word was God." From here we can ponder the deep meaning and depth of prayer that is written into an icon. While Lectio Divina is a method of praying with scripture, Visio Divina (Latin for "divine seeing") is a method for praying with images.

Try these simple steps to meditate on the art in this book.

- Take a few moments to open your heart and mind to God. When you are ready, slowly look and notice the image, taking your time to let feelings and thoughts come to you as you take in forms, figures, colors, lines, textures, and shapes. What does it look like or remind you of? What do you find yourself drawn to? What do you like and not like? What are your initial thoughts? What feelings are evoked?

- Notice these responses without judgment or evaluation.

- As your prayer deepens, open yourself to what the image might reveal to you. Does it arouse for you important meanings or values, remind you of an important event or season, or suggest a new or different way of being?

- Take the time to respond to God in ways matching with your prayer: gratitude, supplication, wonder, lament, confession, song and praise.

- In the remaining few minutes of your prayer with this image, bring to mind, or jot down in a journal (whatever way is most helpful for you), the insights you want to remember and actions you may want to take. Bring your prayer to a close by resting in God's grace and love.

Holy Veneration

It is important to note that while icons may be venerated, (to honor with a ritual act of devotion) this is not idolatry, which is to worship a physical object as God. For example, in our tradition we venerate the cross on Good Friday, light candles in the Mary Chapel, and kneel and pray before a relic of a saint. These are all ritual acts of devotion that bring us closer to God

The Divine Mercy Image

Maria Faustina Kowalska, known as Saint Faustina, was a nun, mystic and visionary in Poland at the beginning of the 20th century. On February 22, 1931, she reports in her diary of a vision of Christ with a command:

"In the evening, when I was in my cell, I saw the Lord Jesus clothed in a white garment. One hand raised in the gesture of blessing, the other was touching the garment at the breast. From beneath the garment, slightly drawn aside at the breast, there were emanating two large rays, one red, the other pale. In silence I kept my gaze fixed on the Lord; my soul was struck with awe, but also with great joy. After a while, Jesus said to me, **"Paint an image according to the pattern you see, with the signature: Jesus, I trust in You. I desire that this image be venerated, first in your chapel, and [then] throughout the world. I promise that the soul that will venerate this image will not perish. I also promise victory over enemies already here on earth, especially at the hour of death. I myself will defend it as My own glory".***   *Diary of Saint Faustina, 47-48*

In the image described by Saint Faustina, Jesus was depicted with his right hand raised in blessing to mankind, as if saying: "Peace be with you." These are words we hear in the liturgy on the Sunday after Easter. On this Sunday, St. John's Gospel (John 20:19-31) relates the appearance of the resurrected Jesus in the room of the last supper and the institution of the sacrament of reconciliation. In the painting we see the rays of blood and water flowing from the veiled pierced heart of Jesus, and the wounds on his hands and feet, giving witness to the events of Good Friday. The picture of Divine Mercy unites the two gospel events, which is the greatest witness of the merciful love of God for all his people.

The Divine Mercy Icon

In 2010, a generous anonymous donor came forward to commission an original piece of art depicting the Divine Mercy image for Divine Mercy Catholic Church in Faribault, Minnesota. Internationally known iconographer, Fabio Nones, professor of theology and director of the Laboratorio Santi Martiri, was commissioned to create the Divine Mercy Icon.

Professor Nones' commentary upon this creation:
"Jesus is presented standing before a closed room with a locked door. Jesus overcomes our fears. The red cloth draped onto the marble column represents the union of heaven and of earth. Jesus is clothed in the white light of the resurrection, and with His right hand He offers a blessing, and with the left hand He points to His side. From His heart flows red and white rays painted over with gold and silver. The look in His eyes is serene and calm, and He invites everyone to come to Him. His hands and feet have the wounds of the cross. The marble pedestal on which He stands represents His royal dignity, His kingship. The inscription at the top means "Jesus Christ."

Timeline of the Divine Mercy Icon:

- February 22, 1931 - St. Faustina reports a vision of Jesus commissioning her to have a painting made of the image of Jesus.
- April 22, 2001 - Divine Mercy Sunday is celebrated for the first time as a Universal Feast of the Church
- August 18, 2002 - Faribault Catholic Community renamed Divine Mercy Catholic Church
- August 2, 2009 - Dedication of Divine Mercy Catholic Church
- February 22, 2012 – The Icon of the Divine Mercy is unveiled in Divine Mercy Catholic Church on Ash Wednesday
- April 15, 2012 —Dedication of Divine Mercy Icon

Father Kevin Finnegan, raised in the suburbs of Chicago, attended St John Vianney Seminary at the University of St. Thomas. He spent ten years after college engaged in ministry to high school and college ministry through the National Evangelization Teams and St. Paul's Outreach. He attended the St. Paul Seminary and was ordained in 1996. Father Kevin served 15 years at Divine Mercy Parish in Faribault, Minnesota before arriving at Our Lady of Grace, Edina in 2014. Fr. Kevin helped found the Companions of Christ, an association of archdiocesan priests living in community and is the recipient of the Bishop Dudley Award from St. Paul's Outreach.

Paul Swenson has been a professional photographer for over 40 years. He has had the privilege of capturing moments and preserving memories that have touched the hearts of generations now and those to come. His eye for artistry, along with his technical skills has not gone unnoticed. Paul is a photographer recognized for advanced education, photographic competition, and service recipient of numerous regional, state, and national awards. "I have been truly blessed with a gift of photography and to give people moments in time to cherish." Paul and his wife Christa, along with their two sons, David and Patrick, live in Faribault, Minnesota. He can be reached at paulswensonphotography@gmail.com.

Sharon Wilson is a Catholic speaker and writer who works to bring others to the fullness of God's Mercy. Touched by an experience of the Holy Spirit, Sharon has come to see the beauty of her wounds and the fullness of the life God has chosen for her. It is her mission to share that joy with others. Sharon lives in Faribault, Minnesota with her husband Dave, and with her children Gabe and Courtney. Find more at www.sharonagneswilson.com.

A Walk of Mercy

Made in the USA
Middletown, DE
19 November 2018